T0131481

MIMESIS

PLATO'S DOCTRINE OF ARTISTIC IMITATION
AND ITS MEANING TO US

PHILOSOPHIA ANTIQUA
A SERIES OF MONOGRAPHS ON ANCIENT PHILOSOPHY

EDITED BY

W. J. VERDENIUS AND J. H. WASZINK

VOLUME III

W. J. VERDENIUS, MIMESIS

LEIDEN
E. J. BRILL
1962

MIMESIS
PLATO'S DOCTRINE OF ARTISTIC IMITATION AND ITS MEANING TO US

BY

W. J. VERDENIUS

Professor of Greek in the University of Utrecht

ONVERANDERDE HERDRUK

LEIDEN
E. J. BRILL
1962

PREFACE

The concept of imitation may be said to be the most vexed problem of Plato's theory of art. No doubt his aesthetics contain more difficulties, but none of them has caused so much misunderstanding. So it may not be amiss to subject this concept to a closer examination from a historical as well as a systematical point of view. An exact interpretation of Plato's doctrine of artistic imitation may not only enlarge and correct our knowledge of his philosophy, but it may also challenge our own reflections on the nature of art. However, it should be borne in mind that the following observations are neither meant as a complete account of Plato's aesthetics nor as an elaborated theory of art.

I am indebted to my colleagues, Professors A. H. Edelkoort, C. J. de Vogel, and J. H. Waszink for some helpful criticisms, and I wish to express my thanks to Dr L. J. Guittart, who once more accepted the unpleasant task of correcting my English.

W. J. V.

CHAPTER I

PLATO'S DOCTRINE OF ARTISTIC IMITATION

It is well known that Plato made imitation the general principle of art. Even music and dance are regarded by him as essentially imitative arts [1]). Aristotle adopted the idea of imitation from his master, and though he modified it in some respects it retained the same fundamental importance in his theory of art. The concept of imitation deeply influenced the aesthetic theories of the Hellenistic and Roman worlds, and it remained the basis for many theories of art as late as the eighteenth century * [2]). Afterwards, under the influence of Romanticism, it became discredited, and this reaction was so strong that at present it still determines the general estimation of Plato's aesthetics. According to Wilamowitz [3]), Plato, in speaking of imitation, "rapped out a fatal word". Many scholars have repeated this condemnation in similar terms. Otto Apelt, for instance, fails to regard the idea of imitation as anything more than "a systematic violation

---

[1]) Cf. *Crat.* 423cd, *Rep.* 399ac, 401a, *Polit.* 306d, *Laws* 655d, 668a, 795e, 798d, 814e.

[2]) The sign * refers to the additional notes at the end of the book.

[3]) *Platon* I² (Berlin, 1920), 479.

of art", "a hunger-cure", "depriving it of all its charms" [1]).

All modern objections against Plato's theory of art centre in the assertion that his rationalism precluded him from recognizing the specific character of artistic creation. He is accused of fashioning art after the pattern of science, which has to copy nature as truly as possible. He is said to have forgotten that true art does not copy an existing reality, but that it creates a new reality arising from the artist's own phantasy, and that it is the spontaneous character of this expression which guarantees the independent value of purely aesthetic qualities. *

However, it may be asked whether this criticism is justifiable from a historical as well as a systematical point of view. In this case two questions arise, firstly, whether Plato really intended imitation to mean a slavish copy, and secondly, whether modern aestheticians are right in disregarding the imitative elements in art and in considering phantasy and self-expression to be its fundamental principles. The first question has an important bearing on the second: for if it should turn out that Plato's concept of imitation is not to be taken in the popular sense, modern aesthetics would seem somewhat rash in proclaiming "that its breaking with the classical doctrine of imitation is irrevocable" [2]). It is to be admitted that this doctrine in the course of history has given rise to

---

[1]) *Platonische Aufsätze* (Leipzig-Berlin, 1912), 68-70.
[2]) F. Leander, *Lessing als ästhetischer Denker*, Göteborgs Högskolas Årsskrift 48 : 3 (1942), 3.

many positions now definitively abandoned. Yet this very fact should induce us to remount to the source of this tradition and to ask ourselves whether the principle in its original enunciation does not deserve some reconsideration.

Such a reconsideration has to be based on a careful examination of the texts. Plato's writings have been called "a veritable poison for chimerical and revolutionary spirits who overlook the qualifications and limitations" [1]. However, for the same reason complacent and conservative spirits are apt to dispose of Plato's thoughts too easily. So let us turn to his own words, with an open mind and attending to their qualifications and limitations.

"Whenever a poet is seated on the Muses' tripod, he is not in his senses, but resembles a fountain, which gives free course to the upward rush of water; and, since his art consists in imitation, he is compelled often to contradict himself, when he creates characters of contradictory moods; and he knows not which of these contradictory utterances is true" (*Laws* 719c) [2].

These words were written down by Plato to illustrate the true nature of the lawgiver by contrasting it with the nature of the artist. So they may create the impression of being no more than a casual remark. However, comparing this passage with Plato's other utterances on the same

---

[1] P. Shorey, *Platonism Ancient and Modern* (Berkeley, 1938), 164.

[2] Quotations from Plato are given in the translations of the Loeb-Library.

subject we seem to be entitled to take it as a starting-point for our discussion, because it can be shown to present the problem in its most radical form.

In his masterly picture of poetic inspiration which is given in the *Io* Plato says: "God takes away the mind of these men, and uses them as his ministers, just as he does soothsayers and godly seers, in order that we who hear them may know that it is not they who utter these words of great price, when they are out of their wits, but that it is God himself who speaks and addresses us through them" (534cd). Evidently inspiration is not a gift freely to be used by the poet, but a compelling force blindly to be followed. Accordingly, the poet's art seems to be completely withdrawn from his will and control. This induces us to interpret his sitting on the tripod of the Muse mentioned above in a more literal sense than our modern outlook might be inclined to do. Exactly like the Delphic priestess he opens himself so fully to his Muse that her inspiration pervades him entirely and takes complete possession of him.

However, if it is the Muse herself who speaks through his mouth, it seems strange that the poet should involve himself in contradictions. There is no room for assuming a malignant intent on the part of the Muse, for Plato expressly assures that "from every point of view the divine and the divinity are free from falsehood", and that" God is altogether simple and true in deed and word, and neither changes himself nor deceives others by visions or words or the sending of signs in waking or in dreams"

(*Rep.* 382e). We can only conclude that the artist himself is to blame for confusing the inspiration of the Muse. This means that his state of being possessed is not absolute: the Muse does not completely direct his tongue and he does not completely lose his human character. Plato stresses the poet's dependence, but he certainly did not mean to represent him as no more than a speaking-tube in the mouth of the Muse. After all, he calls the poet her interpreter (*Io* 534e). Divine inspiration cannot reach the human world but through the poet's interpretation. Accordingly, a poem, though its origin lies beyond human control, does not mechanically reproduce a divine message, but it is the result of a contact in which divine as well as human activities are involved. Interpretation, the human aspect of the process of artistic creation, is easily attended by misunderstanding. The poet is a less able "maker" than his Muse (*Laws* 669c). So if a work of art shows contradictions, this is an imperfection to be imputed to human weakness.

It might be asked whether the occurrence of contradictions in a poem necessarily proves the poet to be confused and his work to be imperfect. Plato says: "The poet contradicts himself, when he creates characters of contradictory moods". If this restriction is taken into account, the poet seems to be free from all blame. In fact, the contradictions between the characters of a piece of literature not only need not impair the unity and the harmony of the whole, but they may even be regarded as necessary means to lend some variety to the work.

However, this argument overlooks an important fact [1]).
The Greeks were inclined to regard their great poets as
reliable sources and infallible authorities for all kinds
of practical wisdom. They isolated the words and deeds
of the epic and tragic characters from their contexts and
used them as general maxims. For instance, the Athen-
ians claimed the high command of an expedition against
the Persians by referring to the *Iliad* (2, 552-554), where
the Athenian Menestheus is said to be unequalled in
drawing up horses and soldiers (Hdt. VII 161). Mytholo-
gical examples were also adduced to excuse actual
wrongdoing, and this practice must have been rather
common, because it is parodied by Aristophanes (*Nub.*
1079-82) and sharply criticized by Plato (*Rep.* 377e-378b,
391d-392a, *Laws* 941b).

In the light of this criticism we can understand Plato's
stressing the contradictory character of poetical variety.
He opposes the Greek inclination towards a pragmatical
interpretation of literature by exposing the poet's lack
of well-founded knowledge. "The poet does not know
what he is saying" (*Apol.* 22bc, *Meno* 99cd, *Tim.* 72a,
Laws 801bc), i.e., the same ecstasy which enables him to
enter into contact with the Muse does not allow him
fully to realize the purport of his own words. Being ab-
sorbed in a flow of successive impressions he is unaware
of their general connections and implications, for his

---

[1]) For a fuller discussion of this problem, see my papers, *L'Ion de
Platon*, Mnemos. III 11 (1943), 233-262, and *Platon et la poésie*,
ib. 12 (1944), 118-150.

state of possession precludes him from passing an independent judgment on the images which present themselves to his mind. He can only register these images
without deliberately arranging them into a well-con-
sidered whole. So the relative character of their contradictions is not sufficiently brought out, and the hearer
is left entangled in a multitude of conflicting views.
This situation is likely to back up his sceptical attitude
of mind, tempting him to choose his poetical pretexts
according to his own interests. It must be admitted that
the poet may at times hit upon a valuable thought (*Rep.*
377a, *Laws* 682a). Yet his work as a whole cannot be
relied upon as a faithful image of truth (*Rep.* 600e).
Even the greatest poetry remains enigmatic (*Alc.* II
147b, *Rep.* 332b, *The.* 194c), for owing to the irrational
origin of his wisdom it is impossible to call the poet to
account about the real meaning of his words (*Hipp. min.*
365d, *Prot.* 347e). So it seems wisest to abstain from definite interpretations (*Lys.* 214b, *Phdr.* 252b, *Rep.* 331e).

This conclusion might seem surprising to the Christian
point of view. A Muse who condescends to so completely
taking possession of her servant should be expected in
some way to guarantee a correct understanding of her
revelations [1]). It would be difficult to give a generally

---

[1]) Cf. G. Finsler, *Platon und die Aristotelische Poetik* (Leipzig,
1900), 185: „Natürlich ist es falsch, an eine Offenbarung zu den-
ken... Mit einer Offenbarung würde es doch schlecht überein-
stimmen, dass den Dichtern nur ein Stück der Wahrheit, höchstens
eine richtige Vorstellung zuteil wird, und dass sie nicht hinlänglich
geeignet sind, das Gute und sein Gegenteil zu erkennen".

accepted definition of Christian revelation. Yet the Christian ideas of revelation may be said to have a common
feature in being based upon the principle of divine love.
The love of God would not be absolute, if it did not to a
certain extent embrace our understanding of its mani-
festations. In this respect it is interesting to compare the
inspiration of the Platonic poet with that of the Old-
Testamentary prophets. These men, too, were seized and
overwhelmed by a divine message and felt themselves
under a compelling force. But this force at the same time
makes a moral demand, which appeals to the deepest
layers of their personality. This appeal does not have an
abstract character, but it is supported by a personal care:
the prophet feels his God to be near to him saying:
"Do not fear, for I am with you to protect you" (Jerem.
1, 8). Thus divine revelation takes the form of a personal
meeting, and this deeply affects the character of human
understanding. The nearness of God is answered by the
confidence of the prophet, who does not waver about the
meaning of his inspirations, but simply puts his trust in
them. Neither his audience need be troubled by episte-
mological doubts: the prophet is an elected being and as
such infallible, though his words may have a further-
reaching, e.g. a messianic, tenor which he did not fully
realize himself [1]).

The Platonic Muse, however, being a true Greek god,
does not know about love. Having touched the poet's

---

[1]) Cf. J. Hessen, *Platonismus und Prophetismus* (Munich, 1939),
52 ff.

mind in its ecstasy, she does not care about the further adventures of her message. The poet can only meet his god when being in an abnormal state, and this god leaves him as soon as he returns to sanity. So he is not only entirely left to himself as to the real meaning of the revelation, but his interpretation is a mere guess, because it refers to something fundamentally inaccessible to rational understanding. *

Accordingly, Plato admonishes his readers to distrust any interpretation of poetry. However, it has already been noted that this warning is mainly directed against the practice of eliciting paradigmatical truths from the great poets. Consequently, it must not be supposed that Plato should have utterly despaired of understanding anything of a poem. The question arises how far his doubts upon the possibility of a pragmatical interpretation are counterbalanced by a belief in the possibility of an aesthetical interpretation. Plato likes to disguise his theoretical views by his pedagogical zeal, and so his theory of art is continually coloured by his solicitude for the mental health of his contemporaries. This fact has caused serious misunderstandings. It has often been denied that Plato held a doctrine, i.e. a systematical opinion, of art, and that his discussion of the cultural function of art is based on a theoretical interpretation. * However, doubts upon this fact have mainly arisen from the modern point of view that systematical knowledge should also be enunciated in a systematical form. Plato does not expound his aesthetics in a systematical form, but the same applies to the whole of his philosophy.

For instance, a recent discussion of Plato's theology has taken the form of "a variety of approaches", and the author rightly observes that (1) "Plato approaches the problem of the nature and activities of the Deity in a variety of ways", (2) "Strictly speaking, however, he did not in the passages which we have examined "approach" the religious problem as such. He discussed other subjects, such as the nature of Being, the nature of the Universe, the status of Soul", (3) "No attempt is discernible to coordinate the different aspects of the theological problem in a comprehensive and unified theory", (4) "We should overstate our case, however, if we refused to find any continuity at all in Plato's successive attacks on the problem" [1]). The same applies to Plato's aesthetics. His approaches to the problem of art are seldom concerned with art as such and his educational interest is seldom absent. But it does not follow that his criticisms should not also have a philosophical aim. This aim is mostly hidden by other arguments and it can only be reconstructed by combining many scattered passages.

What is the aesthetical meaning of Plato's conception of inspirational knowledge? In the *Io* it is only said that the poet is out of his senses, that he is in an ecstasy, and that he is possessed by the Muse (533e-534d), but Plato does not go into a psychological examination of this mental state. He probably adhered to the traditional belief in the divine character of inspiration. * He only states that ecstasy is a prerequisite for artistic quality

[1]) F. Solmsen, *Plato's Theology* (Ithaca, N.Y., 1942), 131, 161.

and that it cannot be replaced by a rational method: "All the good epic poets utter all those fine poems not from art, but as inspired and possessed, and the good lyric poets likewise". "For a poet is a light and winged and sacred thing, and is unable ever to indite until he has been inspired and put out of his senses, and his mind is no longer in him: every man, whilst he retains possession of that, is powerless to indite a verse or chant an oracle" (*Io* 533e, 534b). The same view is expressed in the *Phaedrus* (245a): "He who without the divine madness comes to the door of the Muses, confident that he will be a good poet by art, meets with no success, and the poetry of the sane man vanishes into nothingness before that of the inspired madman". Accordingly, Plato stresses the fact that a true poet should not compose "arguments", but "tales" (*Phd.* 61b).

These passages are important, because they show that Plato knew how to distinguish good poetry from bad poetry, i.e., that he knew how to conceive of poetry in purely aesthetic terms. This is borne out by many other facts: his writing verse in youth, his many quotations from Greek poetry, the poetical quality of his prose, his avowal of "a certain love and reverence for Homer that has possessed me from a boy" (*Rep.* 595b), and his admission of "being under the spell of poetry" (*Rep.* 607c). *

Now, if Plato was able to judge a poem from an aesthetical point of view, he is not likely to have confined himself to emphasizing the irrational origin of inspiration; we also expect him to have explained the character of poetical expression. However, instead of an explanation he presents us with a paradox. In the passage which formed our starting-point the poet is said to contradict himself, "since his art consists in imitation". Would it not be much more natural, if he contradicted himself in spite of the fact that he uses the method of imitation? However, we have seen that (1) these contradictions arise from the fact that the poet's interpretation necessarily confuses the Muse's inspiration, and (2) imitation is the basis of art. It follows that confusion does not take place in spite of imitation, but that it forms an essential characteristic of imitation.

If our assumption that Plato held a systematical doctrine of art is true, it must be possible to give a further definition of this confused character of imitation. The degree of confusion obviously depends upon the artist's familiarity with his object. "It is plain to all that the imitative tribe will imitate with most ease and success the things amidst which it has been reared, whereas it is hard for any man to imitate well in action what lies outside the range of his rearing, and still harder in speech" (*Tim.* 19d). This is a simple thought, but it has important consequences. The poet imitates human characters and he is guided by the Muse. Why this guidance? Obviously because the Muse wants him to express something more than the facts of everyday life in their casual succession. If this were the only aim of his art, imitation would never fail. That it does fail, is an indication that it also refers to something not directly observable and describable, to a more general aspect of reality. Evidently it is the task of the poet to represent these general values through the medium of human life. Imitating characters and actions he must at the same time try to evoke an idea of their ultimate principles. These lie so far from his natural range of thought that he needs the help of divine inspiration. Unfortunately, the ecstatical condition which brings him into contact with the Muse also precludes him from fully understanding her intentions. He can only register his impressions, or in other words, imitate the images which present themselves to his mind. Consequently, his representations are lacking in articulateness: they remain tentative suggestions, in which the general and the particular, the abstract and the concrete, the essential and the accidental are blended so much that the work taken as a whole appears to be inconsistent.

It follows that poetical imitation cannot be a copy true to nature. It remains confused and defective, because it refers to an object with which it is only partly familiar. Imitation implies transformation, and transformation implies confusion, if it is determined by a sphere of reality (in this case, the poetical mind) inferior to its object. This conception has its roots in the general spirit of Plato's philosophy. The world is called a divine work of art (*Tim.* 28a-29a, 37c). As such it is an "image" of something else (29b, 92c), an imitation of a superior model (48e). From these passages it is apparent that the concept of imitation has a metaphysical foundation. This foundation is explained in the tenth book of the *Republic*, where reality is divided into three levels, viz. the ideal Forms, visible objects, and images. A painter is unable to contribute anything to the creation of ideal Being, for he is a human being and bound to the laws of relative reality. Neither may he construct a material object after an ideal pattern, for this is the task of the craftsman. He is forced to descend another step from the realm of ideal Being and to use the visible objects as models for his images. Thus these images are situated on the lowest level of reality, and they are two grades away from the essential nature of things (*Rep.* 596a-597e).

This conclusion does not seem very edifying. Would it really have been Plato's intention to appoint no other task to the painter than copying domestic utensils? Is it conceivable that he, who expresses his admiration for the idealistic art of Phidias (*Meno* 91d) and who is so far from adopting a flat realism in his own literary work, should have refused to painting admittance to the realm of ideal values?

Fortunately, Plato also strikes a different note. The true artist tries to trace the essence of beauty and gracefulness (*Rep.* 401c), and when he has depicted a pattern of the most beautiful man, such an image refers to an ideal the actual occurrence of which is irrelevant (*Rep.* 472d). According to P. Shorey [1]), Plato is here speaking from the point of view of ordinary opinion, and many similar attempts have been made to deny to Plato a sense

[1]) Cf. the note to his translation of *Rep.* 472d in the Loeb-Library.

of idealistic art. * The following interpretation is intended to show that Plato's idealistic conception of art is compatible with his conviction that painting cannot be a direct reflection of ideal Being.

We have already seen that poetry tries to translate a divine message into human language. Similarly, painting both refers to an ideal pattern and a phenomenal image. Though Plato does not explain the relation between the divine character of inspiration and the ideal character of patterns [1]), he expressly declares poetry and painting to be of a similar nature in so far as both are two removes from true reality (*Rep.* 597e, 598e ff.). So their characteristics are to a certain extent mutually applicable. Poetry is said to "imitate human beings acting under compulsion or voluntarily, and as a result of their actions supposing themselves to have fared well or ill and in all this feeling either grief or joy" (*Rep.* 603c), i.e., poetry, just like painting, uses visual reality as a model. But a poet can also be an "imitator of the good" (*Rep.* 397d), and in that case his art obviously gets an idealistic character.

How are we to reconcile these two points of view? It has been suggested that in Plato's own soul idealism and realism fought an unconscious struggle, so that now one power emerged and now the other, and he imperceptibly involved himself in contradictions [2]). Such a psychologic-

---

[1]) An extension of the doctrine of inspiration to painting does not originate until the Hellenistic period, cf. B. Schweitzer, *Der bildende Künstler und der Begriff des Künstlerischen in der Antike*, Neue Heidelb. Jbb. (1925), 28-132.

[2]) *Platonische Aufsätze*, 67.

al explanation might on the face of it seem attractive, because the contradictions, once they are stowed away in the depth of the soul, are removed from our field of vision and easily forgotten. However, this solution of the paradox will hardly satisfy anyone who is convinced of Plato's having a well-balanced personality. This conviction induces us to seek for another interpretation and to validate the importance of Plato's idealistic view of art by connecting it with his general sphere of thought.

The clue to a correct understanding of Plato's philosophy lies in his conception of a hierarchical structure of reality. * There are different planes of being, each of them (except the Good, which is absolutely real) trying, within its own limits, to express the values superior to it. Consequently, the degree of reality of anything is dependent upon its degree of approximation to eternal Being. The empirical world does not represent true reality, but is only an approximation to it, "something that resembles real being but is not that" (*Rep.* 597a), it "yearns" to be like the ideal Forms but "falls short" of them (*Phd.* 74d, 75ab), "with difficulty" it reveals something of the superior world of which it is an "image" (*Phdr.* 250b).

The term "image" shows that Plato's doctrine of imitation is closely related to his hierarchical conception of reality. In fact, "the idea of imitation is at the centre of his philosophy" [1]). Our thoughts and arguments are imitations of reality (*Tim.* 47bc, *Crit.* 107bc), words are

---

[1]) A. Diès, *Autour de Platon* (Paris, 1927), 594.

imitations of things (*Crat.* 423e-424b), sounds are imitations of divine harmony (*Tim.* 80b), time imitates eternity (*Tim.* 38a), laws imitate truth (*Polit.* 300c), human governments are imitations of true government (*Polit.* 293e, 297c), devout men try to imitate their gods (*Phdr.* 252cd, 253b, *Laws* 713e), visible figures are imitations of eternal ones (*Tim.* 50c), etc.

This is sufficient proof that Platonic imitation is bound up with the idea of approximation and does not mean a true copy [1]). Plato himself has warned us against this interpretation: "The image must not by any means reproduce all the qualities of that which it imitates, if it is to be an image". "Do you not perceive how far images are from possessing the same qualities as the originals which they imitate? Yes, I do" (*Crat.* 432bd). In other words, imitation can never be more than suggestion or evocation [2]).

We can now proceed to the question what is the character of artistic suggestion. It cannot directly refer to the ideal values, for art is separated from the plane of real Being by the domain of phenomenal reality. So it must content itself with representing visual objects, it must even humble itself before material reality, in so far as it cannot produce anything but bloodless images. Yet we have seen that true art is inspired by a divine voice

---

[1]) As is maintained e.g. by E. Bignami, *La poetica di Aristotele e il concetto dell' arte presso gli antichi* (Florence, 1932), 128-9.

[2]) Cf. R. Schaerer, *La question platonicienne* (Neuchâtel, 1938), 163 n. 1.

and that it refers to an ideal pattern of beauty. Now the hierarchical structure of reality prevents the ideal Forms from directly manifesting themselves in visual bodies. Beauty itself will not be found "presented in the guise of a face or of hands or of any other portion of the body, nor as a particular description or piece of knowledge, nor as existing somewhere in another substance, such as an animal or the earth or sky or any other thing; but existing ever in singularity of form independent by itself" (*Symp.* 211ab). Correspondingly, the Muse never completely descends to the human level, but to a certain extent she keeps her secret. To a certain extent, for Platonic transcendence is mitigated by the idea of exemplariness. The Demiurge "being devoid of envy desired that all should be, so far as possible, like unto Himself" (*Tim.* 29e). So a gradually fading sheen of eternal radiance may be said to pervade all stages of reality.

Accordingly, art is not confined to the limits of its visual models. True art does not lapse into flat realism, but it strives to transcend the material world; in its poor images it tries to evoke something of that higher realm of being which also glimmers through phenomenal reality. It is true that Plato attaches much value to the likeness of a work of art, but this idea should not be interpreted in modern terms. In true art likeness does not refer to commonplace reality, but to ideal Beauty [1]).

---

[1]) Cf. *Laws* 668b: ἔχουσαν τὴν ὁμοιότητα τῷ τοῦ καλοῦ μιμήματι. I take this much disputed phrase to mean: "which gets its likeness from its being a representation of Beauty".

This carries us back to the confused character of poetical imitation. The above discussion will have shown that the deficiencies of poetry, though they are exaggerated by Plato for his pedagogical purpose, are closely bound up with the ontological status of art in general. Like painting, poetical imitation lies on a lower level of reality than its object, of which it can only produce an adumbration. It tries to transcend itself, but is hampered by the inadequacy of its means. This incommensurability of means and ends causes poetry to approach to divination. But the same holds good of art in general; music, for instance, is said to be full of "guessing" (*Phil.* 56a, 62c).

Art, therefore, has a double aspect: in its visible manifestation it is a thing of the most inferior value, a shadow; yet it has an indirect relation to the essential nature of things. The intensity of this relation depends upon the degree to which the artist succeeds in illuminating the higher aspects of the intermediate plane, viz. of visual reality. Thus imitation, when viewed in the light of a hierarchical conception of reality, may constitute a reconciliation of realism and idealism in art.

This doctrine is well illustrated by the spirit of Greek art. It has been argued that the Greek artist only aimed at deceptive imitation of nature, but that his inner being unconsciously and against his own prejudice bestowed an idealistic character on his work. In this respect, it is said, the practice of art was in advance of the theory of art. The Greek mind, in spite of its gift for idealistic art,

remained unconscious of the fact that true idealism
should abandon given reality [1]).

However, the term "abandon" is out of place here. It
is true that the Greek artist followed nature, but he did
not stick to its casual aspects; he rather tried to detect
its deeper meanings. He was well aware of the fact that
the essential nature of things is not identical with their
visual appearance, but that it must still be represented
in natural forms. He also knew that suggesting a deeper
meaning is not to be achieved through deforming nature
but through clarifying its fundamental structure. So
there is no reason to assume a contrast between artistic
production and aesthetic consciousness. The masters of
Greek idealistic art would have subscribed to Plato's
aesthetics [2]).

Greek art in Plato's time, however, was showing an in-
creasing tendency towards realism, and it is not to be
wondered at that he had serious worries about it. * He
sharply criticizes illusionistic art, which through a skilful
use of perspective and polychromy tries to create the
impression of a second original. This kind of imitation
is denounced as imposture and jugglery (*Rep.* 598d, 602d),
because it claims to produce a doublet of its object. Only
a god could make a doublet of a living being (*Crat.* 432bc).

---

[1]) Bignami, *op. cit.*, 175, H. J. M. Broos, *Plato's beschouwing van
kunst en schoonheid* (Leyden, 1948), 13 n. 19, G. J. Hoogewerff
Verbeelding en voorstelling. De ontwikkeling van het kunstbesef[2]
(Amsterdam, 1944), 43.

[2]) Cf. R. G. Steven, *Plato and the Art of his Time*, Class. Quart.
27 (1933), 153.

Man cannot extend the existing whole of things and so is unable to create anything. Accordingly, true artistic representation does not aim at a deceptive reproduction of the outer appearance of its object, but it is based on a profound study of the real proportions and colours (*Soph.* 233e-236c, *Laws* 668de).

It may be concluded that there are two points differentiating good art from mere trickery: its truthfulness and its modesty. The artist should not content himself with a superficial glance at his object, but he must try to penetrate its inner structure. His task is faithful interpretation, not slavish imitation. Secondly, he should have the honesty to admit the poorness of his means and not try to overstep the limitations they lay upon him. His work should clearly show that its representation of reality, in spite of, or rather, on account of, its very faithfulness, is fundamentally different from reality itself. It should present itself, not as a copy, but as a transposition on a different level and as obedient to the laws of this medium.*

We are now able to understand what it means when art is called a "play" (e.g. *Rep.* 602b, *Soph.* 234ab, *Polit.* 288c, *Laws* 796b, 889de). In Plato's thought this term does not refer to an arbitrary pastime or a mere discharge of surplus energy, but it denotes "every activity which is exercised with a view to something more important" [1]. Accordingly, art does not have its end in itself, but it is only relatively important, in so far as its suggestive power refers to a higher plane of reality. The illusionistic artist

---

[1] Schaerer, *op. cit.*, 22 n. 1.

is not contented with such a subservient role, he attempts "seriously to imitate all things" (*Rep.* 397a) and he is "eager to abandon himself to the fashioning of phantoms and sets this in the forefront of his life as the best thing he has" (*Rep.* 599a).

It should be remembered that Plato does not level his criticism at contemporary art as such, but in so far as it exemplifies a danger resident in art in general [1]). In a sense every artist is unable to recognize the "playing" and relative character of his works. The reason lies in the fact that "he has nothing more valuable than the things he has composed or written" (*Phdr.* 278d), i.e., he does not know a standard of true being which might point out to him the real place of his products in the order of things. Art is called by Plato a "waking dream" (*Soph.* 266c). The nature of the dream state, "whether the man is asleep or awake", lies in "the mistaking of resemblance for identity" (*Rep.* 476c). The artist, who so intensely absorbs himself in his subject matter that "his soul supposes herself to be among the scenes he is describing" (*Io* 535b), is likely to forget the cleavage which separates him from reality and to claim a greater independence for his images than they deserve. * Even if he should deliberately reject a slavish realism and should sincerely attempt to evocate the deeper background of things, his very need of self-transcendence makes him run the risk of taking himself too seriously. The ideal artist, though bestowing serious labours on his work, would not attach

---

[1]) Schaerer, *op. cit.*, 208.

much value to his imitations. In fact, "if he had genuine knowledge of the things he imitates he would far rather devote himself to real things than to the imitation of them" (*Rep.* 599b). So he would frankly admit the deficiencies of his knowledge and his means and would give his products for what they are: images which, by interpreting the real nature of their objects, try to suggest something of the world of ideal Being, but which never belie their irrational origin and the limitations of their medium.

However, Plato realizes very well that such a combination of self-transcendence and humbleness must be a rare thing. Hence he warns his readers to keep a guarded attitude against all art (*Rep.* 608ab, *Laws* 669bc). The spell of imitation may easily overtake us, so that we abandon ourselves to unreliable authorities. This risk is taken by Plato very seriously: "What shall it profit a man if he gain the whole world of poetry and art, and lose his own soul?" (*Rep.* 607d). For art "seems to be a corruption of the mind of all those who do not possess as an antidote a knowledge of its real nature" (*Rep.* 595b).

CHAPTER II

THE MESSAGE OF PLATONIC IMITATION

It might seem a rather bold enterprise to show that Plato's doctrine of artistic imitation still matters to us. Its conclusion, which regards art as a source of mental corruption only to be neutralized by knowledge of its real nature, leaves the impression of a fatal return to the educationalistic position, and not many of us would agree with such a narrowing down of the artist's task. However, Plato's conception of art was not limited to the educational point of view. His warnings against the dangers of artistic representation are also intended to hold good for purely aesthetical enjoyment. When appreciating art we should never forget its limitations.

Yet this conclusion, too, is likely to meet with modern objections. For instance, a recent book on poetics is based on the contention that a pure appreciation of art is possible only if no question is raised about the character of art. The mere intention to ask such a question, even the mere consciousness of the possibility of a theoretical, i.e., a non-artistic, approach to art is said to falsify our appreciation. The same writer argues that the essence of art is inaccessible to scientific determination and that such a determination must acquiesce in the negative conclusion that the relation of artistic to non-artistic reality is inexplicable in rational terms [1]). It may be asked whether this argument is not self-contradictory. An aesthetician who argues that the essence of art is inaccessible to scientific determination pronounces a general statement about art. It seems impossible to pronounce a general statement about any object without having a theoretical approach to that object. However, the same statement presupposes an insight into the essence of art. But by what other method could this insight be attained than by true appreciation? Artistic appreciation is said to be true appreciation so long only as it is free from theoretical by-thoughts. Consequently, at the moment that the art-lover turns into a scientific aesthetician, he loses his contact with the essence of art. How, then, could such an aesthetician venture to give a definition, although a negative definition, of art?

It might be objected that the scientific aesthetician does not want to give a negative definition of art, but only declares himself to be unable to give any true definition of art. He admits that his scientific analysis is never adequate to the artistic phenomenon itself. But in using the word "never" he oversteps the limits of a personal confession, for what he really wants to say is that science as such cannot penetrate into the essence of art, which amounts to a negative definition of art.

It seems impossible that this negative conclusion should automatically spring from the collision of scientific con-

---

[1]) E. G. Wolff, *Aesthetik der Dichtkunst* (Zürich, 1944), 19 ff.

cepts and artistic feeling. In order to give a negative definition of art it is not sufficient to state that the scientific and the artistic approaches to art are different, but
it is necessary to compare their values. The fact that such
a comparison is possible, shows that there must be points
of contact between artistic feeling and rational thinking.
I shall not try to give a definition of these points of
contact. Yet the conclusion seems to be warranted that
true appreciation of art may be accompanied by theoretical considerations. When artistic appreciation is ranked
higher than scientific determination, it is tacitly assumed
that this confrontation, though it brings the artistic
approach into contact with a non-artistic approach, does
not impair its pureness. If it did, the preference of artistic
appreciation would not be based on a true appreciation
of art.

We may even go further and ask ourselves whether a
certain degree of theoretical consciousness is not a necessary precondition to true appreciation. We are told
that an artist cannot but conceive of reality as an artistic
reality, that such a conception excludes any knowledge
of a non-artistic reality (and hence also any comparison
of artistic execution and non-artistic subject-matter),
and that accordingly artistic appreciation is free from
non-appreciative considerations, even from the recognition of a particular work as a work of art, but immediately
arises from its phenomenal aspect as such [1]). However,

---

[1]) Wolff, *op. cit.*, 19, 21, 40-41, 201-202. More instances of this
view are mentioned by J. Hospers, *Meaning and Truth in the Arts*
(Chapel Hill, 1946), 201 n. 59, who rightly remarks that we" can
never forget entirely that there *is* an outside world".

in that case artistic creation and artistic appreciation would require a mental attitude ignoring all things in the world except the work of art with which they are concerned. Such a state of complete absorption seems to run counter to common experience in so far as neither the artist nor the art-lover can unfold their activities without realizing that they are concerned with a specific phenomenon, viz. art. The history of art and the history of criticism are sufficient proof that this realization of being concerned with a specific phenomenon exists and that in many cases it even develops into some idea of what art ought to be. Consequently, Plato seems to be right in his contention that a true appreciation of a work of art presupposes a certain degree of theoretical consciousness as to the nature of art in general.

It is about this general nature of art that many modern philosophers disagree with Plato's view. So we must treat this point at greater length. Plato never tires of emphasizing the limitations of art. In his opinion art does not possess any independent value in the sense of having its aim in itself. It is important only in so far as it points to something more important. It derives its right of existence from a higher standard founded in a more essential realm of being of which it is an indirect reflection, a shadowy image. Art is relative also in this sense that its means are doomed to fall short of its ends: though transcending itself it never grasps the object in its fullness. Every work of art is allegorical: it always expresses something different from what it wants to say.

In short, art cannot be autonomous creation, but at most
tentative interpretation [1]).

These characterizations seem to amount to a radical
dethronement of art which at first sight does not satisfy
us. Two objections have been raised in this connection.
Plato gives art a place in the same hierarchical scale of
realities as ideal being and the phenomenal world, so
that its self-transcending function refers to objects which
are only fully grasped by factual knowledge and philosophical insight. This has been regarded as an intellectualistic deformation of art. For instance, Plato's conception
of a painting as a thing which is two removes from true
reality is said to be based on the naive supposition that
the purpose of a painting is the same as that of its visual
model (e.g. a real bed)—"only under this assumption
could it pertinently be called a reproduction or a copy.
The painting, however, is not at all a second or a third
bed; it is, in all respects, a *painting*". "It should also
be noted that, if 'the excellence or beauty or truth of
every structure, animate or inanimate, and of every
action of man, is relative to the use for which nature or
the artist has intended them' (*Rep.* 601d), then it is not
permissible to condemn a painting as an inferior *substitute*
for a bed; for, it was never intended to serve as such".
"After all, Plato, having made an unsound premise,
still drew a sound conclusion: if art is only appearance,
it is definitely condemned" [2]). These sentences reflect

---

[1]) Cf. also Schaerer, *La question platonicienne*, 158-159.
[2]) F. O. Nolte, *Art and Reality* (Lancaster, 1942), 107, 108, 113.

the general misunderstanding of Plato's controversial intentions which I have tried to refute in the preceding chapter. Plato does not conceive of imitation as a slavish copy and he does not condemn art as a substitute for real being, but he condemns those artists and those interpreters who take artistic "images" to be equivalent to reality. * So he does not contradict himself when he claims to have defined art in accordance with the use for which it is intended. His whole argument is concentrated upon an attempt to circumscribe the limits of art as such and to assign to it its proper place in the whole of things [1]).

However, though Plato did not regard art as a substitute for other things, he did call it an adumbration of those realities to which factual and philosophical knowledge, too, refer (cf. *Polit.* 277c). It must be admitted that this position savours of the same intellectualism which also induced him to call philosophy "the true Muse" (*Rep.* 548b, cf. *Phd.* 61a, *Laws* 689d, 817bc). Plato did too little justice to the specific functions of aesthetical feeling and emotion, though he did not completely ignore them. For instance, he recognized the importance of "true pleasures" in artistic appreciation (*Phil.* 51b ff.) and of "qualitative proportion" as distinct from mathematical proportion (*Polit.* 284e). * Yet he may be reproached for omitting to determine the relations between the rational and the non-rational aspects of art. But how many modern philosophers have succeeded in this task?

---

[1]) Cf. Schaerer, *op. cit.,* 186-187.

The preceding objection was directed against Plato's intellectualistic conception of the dependent character of art. A second and last objection opposes the idea of dependence itself. I have already remarked that Plato's aesthetics is often censured for putting imitation, instead of expression, at the centre of art. In this connection expression really means self-expression, and "self" refers to the world of imagination. I shall not deal with the place of imagination in art but only discuss the general conception underlying those views which take this factor to be all-important, viz. the conception of art as the creation of an autonomous reality. This doctrine has found its classical expression in Bradley's words: "Poetry may have also an ulterior value as a means to culture or religion; because it conveys instruction, or softens the passions, or furthers a good cause ... But its ulterior worth neither is nor can directly determine its poetic worth as a satisfying imaginative experience; and this is to be judged entirely from within ... For its nature is to be not a part, nor yet a copy, of the real world (as we commonly understand that phrase), but to be a world by itself, independent, complete, autonomous; and to possess it fully you must enter that world, conform to its laws, and ignore for the time the beliefs, aims, and particular conditions which belong to you in the other world of reality" [1].

It cannot be denied that this doctrine has exercised a salutary influence as a reaction against that under-

[1] A. C. Bradley, *Oxford Lectures on Poetry* (London, 1909), 4-5.

estimation which regarded poetry as "the decoration of a preconceived and clearly defined matter" [1]), and that over-estimation which called it "the most beautiful, impressive and widely effective mode of saying things" (Arnold), "the breath and finer spirit of all knowledge" (Wordsworth), "the stuff of which our life is made" (Hazlitt) *, and which carried itself *ad absurdum* in Wilde's saying that "external Nature imitates Art" [2]).

However, the conception of art as a world by itself gives rise to many difficulties, some of which may be mentioned here. In the first place, if artistic value "is to be judged entirely from within", the essence of a work of art is supposed to lie in its inner harmony, i.e., its formal beauty. It has often been said that Beauty is the object of art, and it is not to be wondered at that this view should also have been pronounced as a criticism of Plato [3]). Accordingly, artistic appreciation is said to be confined to the enjoyment of beholding phenomenal forms [4]) or to a "delight in construction itself" [5]). Plato has sounded a warning note against this cult of beauty, which threatens to reduce art to the level of a superficial

---

[1]) This characterization is borrowed from Bradley, *op. cit.*, 23.

[2]) O. Wilde, *Complete Works* (New York, 1927), 63.

[3]) E.g. by C. Ritter, *Die Kerngedanken der platonischen Philosophie* (Munich, 1931), 307.

[4]) Cf. N. Hartmann, *Das Problem des geistigen Seins* (Berlin, 1933), 413, 452, L. W. Beck, *Judgments of Meaning in Art*, Journ. of Philos. 41 (1944), 175: "The phenomenon is all that is needed in art".

[5]) S. Alexander, *Philosophical and Literary Pieces* (London, 1939), 248.

and arbitrary formalism. He flays the shallowness of those minds whose artistic sense can only be enthralled by the play of colours and forms (*Rep.* 601a), and he demands that our appreciation should be focused through the beautiful form on its content (*Laws* 669ab) [1].

We seem to follow his advice when calling a work of art "profound" or "superficial" and when ascribing a definite degree of "insight" to an artist. In that case we use a standard which transcends the realm of imagination and which bears an analogy to the idea of truth. Artistic truth, just as scientific truth, cannot be restricted to internal consistency, but involves a reference to something else which is not art itself. Bradley is right in arguing that the meaning of a work of art cannot be adequately expressed in any language but its own, but he errs in concluding that "it means itself" [2]. A thing which means itself is a *monstrum*, for meaning cannot be defined in terms of self-containment, but always implies a reference to something different from that by which it is meant. Bradley implicitly admits his own contradiction when he remarks that art "still seems to be trying something beyond itself" and that it "refers to, and interprets, reality" [3]. *

The second difficulty affects the idea of creation. It has been remarked that "the real ground why Plato made

---

[1] Aristotle has developed this view, cf. H. L. Tracy, *Aristotle on Aesthetic Pleasure*, Class. Phil. 41 (1946), 43-46, 193-206.

[2] *Op. cit.*, 24-25.

[3] *Op. cit.*, 26, 34.

imitation the essence of art lies in the fact that he did not yet know the notion of creation" [1]). This is true, but is Plato to be censured for "not yet" knowing the notion of creation? Is there no danger in proclaiming the freedom of artistic creation? And is there no wisdom in Plato's warning that a man who claims to have created something absolutely new is to be regarded as a charlatan producing false illusions just as the sophists (*Soph.* 234b, *Rep.* 596c, *Crat.* 432bc)? The history of art seems to give an answer to these questions. Whenever artistic imagination has taken absolute power, freedom has degenerated into caprice, creation into jugglery, and expression into self-idolization. In fact it has too often been forgotten that the artist is not himself a Muse, but a "servant of the Muse", as Plato puts it (*Io* 534c). His freedom is restricted by the fact that he lives in a given world. So he cannot create new realities, but can only try to give new interpretations of reality.

It will at once be objected that there is at least one branch of art where it seems impossible to replace the principle of creation by that of interpretation, viz. music. Here the phenomenal forms are said to have an independent existence, and not to receive their sense from something else. I shall not try to give a systematical defence of the interpretative character of music, but only wish to recall that many great musicians have avowed their being inspired by a wider range of reality.

---

[1]) J. Walter, *Die Geschichte der Aesthetik im Altertum* (Leipzig 1893), 442.

Mozart was very sensitive to the beauty of natural scenery and desired to reproduce these impressions in his work; Beethoven, when asked for an explanation of the *D minor sonata*, replied "Read Shakespeare's *Tempest*"; and Schumann wrote: "I reflect on all that goes on in the world in my own way, and it issues outwards in the form of music". There is no reason to deny that these wider experiences should be more than arbitrary occasions and have a vital importance to the meaning of the musical works themselves. *

There is a second objection against the interpretative conception of art which may be briefly discussed here. It has been argued that works of art are neither mutually compatible nor mutually contradictory, so that they cannot reveal the nature of the actual world, but refer to the sphere of possibility. Accordingly, every work of art is "an isolated self-sufficient structure which often impresses us as being a windowless monad which mirrors a world", an alternative to the actual "which is intrinsically significant and valuable because it is better than the actual" [1]). Let us pass over the question as to the value of possible worlds and ask ourselves whether really "Cézanne's vision of three-dimensional space and of the objects in that space is radically incompatible with the vision of Turner" [2]). Cézanne and Turner may be said

[1]) D. Walsh, *The Cognitive Content of Art*, Philos. Rev. 52 (1943), 438-449.

[2]) *Op. cit.*, 439. On p. 440 it is maintained that in Cézanne's works "the graceful vistas of Watteau's landscapes are not merely absent or neglected; they are specifically rejected". This seems to

to interpret reality from different points of view, and it
is hard to see why these points of view should not be
compatible. It must be admitted that, if they are compatible, "they must be capable of synthesis into larger
more adequate or more inclusive wholes" [1]. There are
many examples of works of art which constitute a synthesis of previous and more one-sided approaches. But
even if such a synthesis cannot be realized in a distinct
work of art, it seems to take place in the mind of the
spectator, in an analogous way as when a tourist who has
had a series of different views of a landscape can combine
them to a general impression in his mind.

Finally, I wish to call attention to a misunderstanding
which has often obscured the true function of art. Art is
rightly said to possess a proper value which cannot be
communicated by other means. In this sense artistic
value may be called "immanent" and "exclusively founded in the work of art itself". However, it does not follow
that a work of art "creates its own significance" in this
sense that "it is itself its own object" and "originates from
itself" [2]. This autarchistic view of art arises from a
confusion of artistic value and artistic meaning which
seems to have been caused by the dual meaning of the

---

run counter to the author's view that works of art are not mutually
contradictory, for a contradiction is said to take place, if "the
acceptance of one must necessitate the rejection of others".

[1] Op. cit., 440.

[2] D. Bartling, De structuur van het kunstwerk (Amsterdam,
1941), 24, 105, 113.

term "significance", viz. (1) importance or value, and (2) reference or signification [1]).

I have argued that Plato's doctrine of artistic imitation is based on the conception of art as an interpretation of reality and that this principle is still a sound basis for our theory of art. This is no new discovery, for the interpretative character of art seems to become more and more recognized in different quarters. * I have only tried to point out that this recognition may save us from serious theoretical difficulties. These difficulties may be summed up as follows: so long as art is considered to be essentially creative, an artistic representation of a natural object must be taken to be at the same time identical with, and different from, this object. *

But also the practice of art may get some benefit from Plato's thoughts. They may help to keep it off a superficial cult of formal beauty as well as off an overstrained desire of originality. I have already spoken about these dangers, but should like to add a few words about

---

[1]) Th. M. Greene, *The Arts and the Art of Criticism* (Princeton, 1940), 229 n. 1, has rightly pointed out this difference. Even B. C. Heyl, *New Bearings in Esthetics and Art Criticism* (New Haven, 1943), who aims "to show in what ways and to what degree linguistic confusion is responsible for the inadequacy of contemporary art criticism and esthetics" (1), seems to confuse artistic value and artistic meaning and to conclude from the immanent character of the former to the immanent character of the latter, when he says: "If works of art are taken as symbols, their artistic meanings or values seem so intimately bound up with the objects themselves that external references and associations are esthetically unwarranted" (84).

the latter. False originality seems to spring from the delusion that artistic creation is almighty. Plato stresses the weakness of art, the poorness of its images. The true artist is conscious of these deficiencies, he knows that he lags behind his object and that he can never fully express its essence. But this very consciousness of producing mere adumbrations of the real nature of things seems to enable him to reveal something of what is behind appearance [1]. Only that servant of the Muses who feels himself "not an inventor, but a translator" [2] will be a master. Only that artist who is convinced of the smallness of his art will create great art. The above reflections on Plato's doctrine of artistic imitation may contribute to this modesty.

---

[1] Cf. also G. van der Leeuw, *Wegen en Grenzen*² (Amsterdam, 1948), 384. However, it does not seem necessary to call any true work of art "religious" for this reason (*ibid.*, 427).

[2] M. Proust, quoted by Schaerer, *op. cit.*, 158 n. 2.

ADDITIONAL NOTES

p. 1   On the influence of the concept of imitation cf. P. Cauer, *Terminologisches zu Platon und Aristoteles*, Rh. Mus. 73 (1920), 161-8; A. Rostagni, *Aristotele e Aristotelismo nella storia dell' Estetico antico*, Stud. It. Fil. 2 (1921), 1-147; S. H. Butcher, *Aristotle's Theory of Poetry and Fine Art*[4] (London, 1923), Ch. II; U. Galli, *La mimesi artistica secondo Aristotele*, Stud. It. Fil. 4 (1924), 314-90; E. Bignami, *La poetica di Aristotele e il concetto dell' arte presso gli antichi* (Florence, 1932), Ch. V; W. F. Trench, *Mimesis in Aristotle's Poetics*, Hermath. 47 (1933), 1-24; R. McKeon, *Literary Criticism and the Concept of Imitation in Antiquity*, Mod. Phil. 34 (1936), 26-35; Craig la Drière, *Horace and the Theory of Imitation*, A.J.P. 60 (1939), 288-300; K. E. Gilbert and H. Kuhn, *A History of Esthetics* (N.Y., 1939), 63-72 and *passim*; R. McKeon, *The Philosophic Bases of Art and Criticism*, Mod. Phil. 41 (1943), 155-6; J. J. Donahue, *The Theory of Literary Kinds. Ancient Classifications of Literature* (Iowa, 1943), Ch. IV; Ph. De Lacy, *Stoic Views of Poetry*, A. J. Ph. 69 (1948), 256 ff.

p. 2   Objections against Plato's doctrine of imitation are raised e.g. by J. Walter, *Die Geschichte der Aesthetik im Altertum* (Leipzig, 1893), 439, 442, 446, 451; F. Stählin, *Die Stellung der Poesie in der platonischen Philosophie* (Nordlingen, 1901), 59-60; J. Adam on *Rep.* 595c; O. Apelt, *Platonische Aufsätze* (Leipzig-Berlin, 1912), 71; E. Zeller, *Die Philosophie der Griechen* II 1[5] (Leipzig, 1922), 936-7; E. Bignami, *La poetica di Aristotele*, 16-17; L. Stefanini *Il problema estetico in Platone*[5] (Turin, 1935), 189-190, 194; A. Fox, *Plato for Pleasure* (London, 1945), 107-8.

p. 9   From the contrast between the Platonic and the Christian conceptions of revelation it should not be concluded that Plato's religious thought should not bear any resemblance to Christianity. An interesting discussion of the similarities and differences is given by R. Schaerer, *Dieu, l'homme et la vie d'après Platon* (Neuchâtel, 1944), 171 ff. The most fundamental point of difference seems to be that Plato, though he believed in a certain solidarity between

God and man (Schaerer, 172-5, 199-200), could not conceive of this contact as a personal meeting (Schaerer, 177-9, 191, 196-7, 207). Consequently, the grace and providence of his God are of an abstract nature (Schaerer, 190, and F. Solmsen, *Plato's Theology* (Ithaca, N.Y., 1942), 151 ff.).

. 9   That Plato's treatment of art is based on a theoretical interpretation has been denied e.g. by Wilamowitz, *Platon* I² (Berlin, 1920), 477: "Das Verdammungsurteil, das der Staat über Homer und auch über die Tragödie fällt, deren Ahnherr er ist, wurzelt gar nicht in dem Wesen der Poesie"; E. Cassirer, *Eidos und Eidolon. Das Problem des Schönen und der Kunst in Platons Dialogen*, Vortr. Bibl. Warburg 1922/3, 26: "Platons System kennt als solches keine philosophische Ästhetik, ja es kennt nicht einmal deren Möglichkeit"; P. Friedländer, *Platon* I (Berlin-Leipzig, 1928), 138: „Eine schlechthin gültige Kunstphilosophie zu entwerfen kam Platon nicht in den Sinn"; H. G. Gadamer, *Plato und die Dichter* (Frankfort, 1934), 12: "Platos Stellung zu den Dichtern ist nicht eine Konsequenz seines Systems". J. W. H. Atkins, *Literary Criticism in Antiquity* I (Cambridge, 1934), 49, argues that his criticism of poetry "takes the form, not of an inquiry based on first principles, but of a sort of special pleading in support of a conviction already arrived at" (viz. that philosophy should be accepted as the guide to truth and conduct). E. Spranger, *Lebensformen* (Halle, 1927), 191, even suggests that Plato's judgment should have been inspired by a personal feeling of inferiority and jealousy with regard to the artists.

10   I cannot agree with G. Finsler, *Platon und die Aristotelische Poetik* (Leipzig, 1900), 185, who maintains: "Die begeisternden Musen und Chariten, wie die inspirierenden Götter überhaupt, sind nicht als reale Potenzen zu fassen, sondern zum poetischen Schmuck aus dem populären Glauben herübergenommen". Similarly, H. Leisegang, *Der Heilige Geist* I 1 (Leipzig, 1919), 194-5, 200, and U. Galli, Stud. It. Fil. 4 (1924), 312, are failing to see in Plato's description of divine inspiration anything more than "a sharp opposition" or "an ironical concession" to current opinion. That his theory should be taken seriously, is rightly pointed out by O. Wichmann, *Platos Lehre vom Instinkt und Genie*, Kantstud. 40. Erg. H. 1917, 62 ff. For the idea of inspiration in antiquity, cf. H. Leisegang, *op. cit.*, 126 ff.; W. Kranz, *Das Verhältnis des Schöpfers*

zu seinem Werk in der althellenischen Literatur, N. Jbb. 53 (1924), 65 ff.; W. Kroll, *Studien zum Verständnis der römischen Literatur* (Stuttgart, 1924), Ch. II; A. Delatte, *Les conceptions de l'enthousiasme chez les philosophes présocratiques* (Paris, 1934); O. Falter, *Der Dichter und sein Gott bei den Griechen und Römern* (Würzburg, 1934); F. Wehrli, *Der erhabene und der schlichte Stil in der poetisch-rhetorischen Theorie der Antike*, Phyllobolia für P. Von der Mühll (Basel, 1946), 11-17, H. F. North, *The Concept of Sophrosyne in Greek Literary Criticism*, Cl. Phil. 43 (1948), 12 ff.

p. 11   Further evidence of Plato's appreciation of poetry is given in my paper *Platon et la poésie*, Mnemos. III 12 (1944), 122-3. In this paper I have tried to show (1) that Plato's personal appreciation of art is compatible with his criticism of its cultural function, and (2) that both this appreciation and this criticism are in accordance with his general philosophy. The present discussion is intended as a corroboration of this view. I cannot agree with K. Popper, *The Open Society and its Enemies* I (London, 1945), 200 n. 39, who maintains that Plato's avowal of his admiration for Homer is only "a concession to the reader's sentiments".

p. 15   That Plato wanted to separate art from ideal beauty, is maintained by E. Cassirer, *Eidos und Eidolon*, 20, and similarly, by U. Galli, Stud. It. Fil. 4 (1924), 299-301. H. J. M. Broos, *Plato's beschouwing van kunst en schoonheid* (Leyden, 1948), 63, arrives at the conclusion: "What stands out in his view is the fundamental difference between art and true beauty". This view is extended to the whole of Greek aesthetics by B. Bosanquet, *History of Aesthetic* (London, 1892), 16, who contends that, according to the Greeks, "artistic representation is no more than a kind of commonplace reality", and by E. Bignami, *La poetica di Aristotele*, 18-19, who holds that "Bello ed Arte ... costituiscono per l'antichità i poli di due mondi distinti ed inconciliabili", and even ventures the conclusion that to the ancients art was "un cadavere". Wilamowitz, *Platon* I, 703, says: "Es muss ausgesprochen werden, dass Plato für die bildende Kunst überhaupt kein Herz gehabt hat, und wenn er ein Auge hatte (was sich nicht leugnen lässt), es mit Absicht verschlossen hat, aus Furcht vor dem schönen Schein", and in note 1: "Auf das, was der Staat 472d sagt, dass der gute Maler einen so schönen Menschen malt, dass er vorbildlich (typisch) wird, ist nicht viel zu geben; das bringt die Gefahr eines leeren "Idealisierens""

mit sich, das gerade dem gesunden Kunstsinn unausstehlich wird".
However, one may ask whether Wilamowitz's conviction of the
dangers inherent in this kind of art warrant us to disregard Plato's
conviction of its eminence. If Plato should have been indifferent
to fine art, would he have called Phidias a man, "who made such
conspicuously beautiful works" (*Meno* 91d)? Cf. also *Rep.* 540c:
"A most beautiful finish, Socrates, you have put upon your rulers,
as if you were a statuary". These passages, as well as *Rep.* 361d,
420c, *Polit.* 277a, refute Jaeger's contention, "Sculpture he ignores"
(*Paideia* II (Oxford, 1944), 228). Broos, *op. cit.*, 17-18, refers to
Rep. 598a; but from the fact that art is no *direct* imitation of the
ideal Forms it does not follow that it could not reveal them in-
directly. Similarly, in *Polit.* 286a Plato says that the ideal Forms
can only be *clearly* revealed by argument, which does not exclude
the possibility of another, though a less ideal, approach. Broos
(*op. cit.*, 16) further adduces *Tim.* 28ab, but this passage does not
imply that a human artist should be compelled to confine his
attention to the changeable aspects of his model. It is true that the
painter mentioned in *Rep.* 472d is an ideal painter, but this does
not mean that he should be "unreal" (Broos, 19). Plato could not
have used this comparison, if his readers had been unable to imagine
idealistic art. Finally, in order to explain Plato's love of art and his
own artistic excellence, Broos says: "He combines the giftedness
of the artist with the contemplativeness of the philosopher, but
not the mentality of 'aesthetic man' with that of 'philosophic
man' " (*op. cit.*, 63). However, I fail to understand such a separation
of artistic talents from aesthetic sensibility (see also p. 20). On
Plato's idealistic conception of art see also R. C. Lodge, *Plato's
Theory of Education* (London, 1947), 221-2. It should be remembered
that this conception has been adopted and elaborated by Aristotle,
cf. *Poet.* 1451b, 5; 1460b, 33; 1461b,9, and Butcher, *Aristotle's
Theory of Poetry and Fine Art*, Ch. III.

16   Plato's hierarchical conception of reality is rightly emphasized
by R. Schaerer, *La question platonicienne* (Neuchâtel, 1938), *La
composition du Phédon*, Rev. Et. Gr. 53 (1940), 1-50, *Dieu, l'homme
et la vie d'après Platon* (Neuchâtel, 1944). I owe very much to these
outstanding works, especially to *La question platonicienne*, 157 ff.
One can only wonder that after the publication of this book it has
been asserted without comment: "There is no trace of such a hie-

rarchy in Plato " (F. Steckerl, Cl. Phil. 37 (1942), 297). For the
following see also R. G. Collingwood, *Plato's Philosophy of Art*,
Mind 34 (1925), 157-8; A. Diès, *Autour de Platon* (Paris, 1927),
594; J. Tate, *Plato and "Imitation"*, Class. Quart. 26 (1932), 164-5;
W. Michaelis in *Theol. Wörterb. z. N. T.* IV (1942), 663.

p. 20   On Plato's criticism of the art of his time cf. R. G. Steven, *Plato
and the Art of his Time*, Class. Quart. 27 (1933), 149-55; P. M.
Schuhl, *Platon et l'art de son temps* (Paris, 1933); T. B. L. Webster,
Greek Art and Literature 530-400 B.C. (Oxford, 1939), 138 ff., 174
ff.; K. Glaser, *Platons Stellung zum Kampfe von Philosophie und
tragischer Dichtung*, Wien. Stud. 58 (1940), 33 ff. I cannot agree with
H. G. Gadamer, *Plato und die Dichter* (Frankfort, 1934), 12, 14-15,
36, who holds that Plato's criticism never concerns the degene-
rating poetry of his own time.

p. 21   On the distinction of two kinds of imitation cf. Schaerer, *La
question platonicienne*, 161-5. I cannot agree with Broos, *Plato's
beschouwing van kunst en schoonheid*, 19 n. 17, that there is only a
gradual difference between them. It is true that all imitations are
images (*Soph.* 265b), and that images are said to possess only a
relative grade of being (*Soph.* 240ab), but this does not mean that
they should necessarily be connected with deception. Broos (note
14) refers to *Soph.* 260c and 264cd. But the first passage only says
that, if deception exists, there will also be images, a statement
which is not reversible. The second statement runs: "There are no
images, if ψεῦδος does not exist". This term is not to be translated
by "falsehood", but it denotes what is not wholly real and yet has
some sort of existence. Cf. 240b, where τὸ ἐοικός is defined as
τὸ μὴ ἀληθινόν, which is explained as οὐκ ὄντως ὄν, ἀλλ' ἔστι γε
μὴν πως.

It has often been maintained that there is a contradiction
between *Rep.* III, where imitation is allowed and even encouraged
(398b, 401b), and *Rep.* X, where imitative poetry is said not to be
admitted into the ideal state (595a). However, in the latter passage
the term imitation is meant in the popular sense of slavish copy, as
is pointed out by J. Tate, *Imitation in Plato's Republic*, Class.
Quart. 22 (1928), 16-23, *Plato and Imitation*, ib. 26 (1932), 161-9.
See also Schaerer, *op. cit.*, 164 n. 2. Aristotle has the same non-
chalance in using a word now in its wider and popular sense and
now as a technical term.

22   H. J. Paton, *Plato's Theory of* εἰκασία, Proc. Arist. Soc. 22 (1922),
69-104, rightly emphasizes the fact that, according to Plato, art
is a kind of dream, but he fails to give a correct interpretation of
this conception, when he writes: "He (the artist) bids farewell to
truth and therefore to falsehood. He does not assert or deny anything, it is impossible to contradict him ... As far as aesthetical
considerations are concerned, it is wholly indifferent to the artist
whether the originals of his εἰκόνες exist or not" (p. 93). Plato
would not have been able to conceive of an "image" of which no
model exists. He would have subscribed to the view that the artist
"is concerned with his object not as an instance of a philosophic
truth, or as a reproduction of an actual fact" (p. 96), but not to
the conclusion that the artist is concerned with his object "as an
appearance and an appearance alone" (p. 97). Every appearance
points to something else, and Plato's aesthetics mainly consist of
an attempt to determine this function of "pointing to" in so far
as it is embodied in artistic representation. Paton is forced to deny
all value to the fact that art is called "imitation": "These are mere
phrases to lead the pupil up to a grasp of the true relation" (p. 102).
But according to his own interpretation mentioned above there
could not be any relation at all. His misconception of the relation
of imitation has led him to a further error, viz. that Plato "is blaming
the artist for not being a scientist or an historian" (p. 100). Some-
times Plato seems to do this indeed, but his real intention was to
oppose those interpreters who took artistic imitation for scientific
or historical truth.

29   It is curious that Nolte himself expresses the correct view on
p. 25: "The primary complaint is, not against poets and artists
as such, but against an arbitrary guild of specialists who had
assumed or had been assigned a comprehensive pedagogical and
practical importance out of all proportion to their particular
qualifications". In a note he refers to the idealistic conception of
art in *Rep.* 472d without trying to connect it with Plato's other
statements. He also calls attention to *Phdr.* 248d, where we are
told that the soul which has seen most of truth shall be incarnated
in the person of a philosopher ἢ φιλοκάλου ἢ μουσικοῦ τινος. However, it is misleading to translate these last words by "artist" and
"musician", and it should also be remembered that in the same
passage the ποιητικὸς ἢ τῶν περὶ μίμησίν τις ἄλλος is put only in the

sixth place. In this connection μουσικός seems to mean "inspired votary of art" (the same meaning is to be assumed in 243a, where it is commonly mistranslated by "lyric poet", "musician", or "educated"). The contrast with common poetry and art is obviously intended to suggest the possibility of a more idealistic kind of art. Cf. also B. Schweitzer, *Mimesis und Phantasia*, Philol. 89 (1934), 289-290.

p. 29   These non-rational elements in Plato's aesthetics are rightly stressed by L. Robin, *Platon* (Paris, 1935), 306-307. Plato is so reticent about the positive value of emotion in art, because he was very apprehensive of the dangers of emotionalism (cf. my paper *Platon et la poésie*, Mnemos. III 12 (1944), 125 ff., R. C. Lodge, *Plato's Theory of Education* (London, 1947), 94-95). So he admitted that art is to be judged according to the pleasure it affords, but he significantly added the qualification "not, however, the pleasure of any chance person" (*Laws* 658e).

p. 31   For references and examples, see R. McKeon, *The Philosophic Bases of Art and Criticism*, Mod. Philol. 41 (1943), 131 ff. The overestimation of the powers of fine art still persists. Cf. e.g. F. R. O' Neill, *The Social Value of Art* (London, 1939), 34: "An artist, as I shall try to show, is the only person who is concerned with the expression and communication of actual complete experience".

p. 32   On artistic truth cf. the excellent work of Th. M. Greene, *The Arts and the Art of Criticism* (Princeton, 1940), 233-234, 424-460. The existence of artistic truth has recently been disputed by S. Zink, *Poetry and Truth*, Philos. Rev. 54 (1945), 132-154. He argues that the qualification "true" when applied to a work of art really means "valuable" (153), and that this value can only lie in its "internal organization" (150), because "poetic statements involve no references; they describe nothing external at all" (144). "The poem is an assembly of qualities which qualify, not an existing object, but each other". "In the poem the appreciator attends to and remains with the connotations of the words; he responds to the meanings as pure meanings, and intensifies and enriches each meaning by exploring its relations to the other meanings taken as pure meanings, as qualities" (142). "The poem as a whole refers to nothing beyond itself; it is the embodiment of an individual quality, and as such possesses no significant relations save those internal to the various parts in which the quality is elaborated" (152). The same view is

defended by the author in his paper *The Poetic Organism,* Journ.
of Philos. 42 (1945), 421-433. Cf. also L. W. Beck, *Judgments of
Meaning in Art,* Journ. of Philos. 41 (1944), 175: "Art which has
a meaning is a sensuous presentation of connotations without
denotations ... meaning without the meant", and H. J. Paton
in Proc. Aristot. Soc. 22 (1922), 97-98: "The excellence of his
(Shakespeare's) work depends upon its own internal structure, and
not upon its resemblance to actual historical events. If there is
any merit in such a resemblance it would be a merit which was
definitely not aesthetic. The only verisimilitude we have a right
to ask from the artist is that his work should be like itself, i.e.,
that it should be internally coherent ... To the artist art is not
the sign of anything other than itself ... just this, this unique and
individual child of his fancy, and nothing else in the whole world".
It is clear that such a view would restrict the value of art to
mere formal beauty, a restriction which does not need any further
refutation. However, it might be asked why this conception of art
should be so persistent in spite of its obvious one-sidedness. The
answer seems to be that many aesthetes have inflated their love
of art to such a fanaticism that they want to keep their god free
from worldly associations at any cost. Ch. W. Morris, *Esthetics and
the Theory of Signs,* Journ. of Unif. Science 8 (1939/40), 130-150,
has tried logically to justify this claim of self-sufficiency. The paradox of an "immanent meaning" of art is solved by the suggestion
that "in esthetic perception value properties are taken account
of both mediately and immediately: mediately in that they are
presented by signs, immediately in that the sign vehicles used
embody in themselves in varying degrees the value properties
which they present" (139). Accordingly, an artistic sign is said
to have "its own sign vehicle among its denotata" (136). However,
we are warned that in aesthetic apprehension the sign vehicle
"must be realized as such", i.e., must be distinguished from the
denotata: "the value must be there for direct inspection and yet
also there as indicated by signs" (137). This qualification induces
us to raise the question whether the value as embodied in the sign
vehicle and as indicated by the sign is really the same value. The
immanent properties of the sign vehicle seem to bear only a formal
similarity to those denoted by the sign. This formal similarity may
easily deceive us so as to suggest that there is a complete identity

and that the meaning of a work of art is exhausted by its visible embodiment. The imitative elements in art have a certain blinding force; they often appear to be so "real" that they are taken to be self-sufficient. So aesthetic purism is based on the same naive acceptance of imitation which it tries to replace.

This criticism also applies to B. C. Heyl, *New Bearings in Esthetics and Art Criticism* (New Haven, 1943), 82 ff., who argues (1) that it is the significance (importance, greatness, profundity) of a work of art which artistically matters, and (2) that this significance should be dissociated from truth in the sense of a correspondence to reality. This dissociation is based on the assumption that artistic meanings are part of the symbols themselves, and it is supported by the argument that what artistically counts is "the imaginitive freshness, the vividness, and the vitality of the conception". However, we do not enjoy these qualities in themselves, but only in so far as they qualify a reference to something else. Such a qualified reference may be called an interpretation.

For a criticism of Bradley's view cf. also I. A. Richards, *Principles of Literary Criticism*[6] (London, 1938), 74 ff., who, however, draws the doubtful conclusion that poetry "is made up of experiences of exactly the same kinds as those that come to us in other ways" (78). Still more questionable seems his view that in poetry these experiences act as "provisional acceptances", which "are held only for the sake of their dramatic effect" (278), so that "all that matters is acceptance, that is to say, the initiation and development of the further response", a response which "need not be directed towards anything to which the statement refers" (273). Similar ideas are enunciated by M. C. Nahm, *Aesthetic Experience and its Presuppositions* (New York, 1946), who argues that "the dominant feeling in aesthetic experience is one of exaltation" (486). "The tendency of the exalted mood of courage is to go beyond the limits imposed for the experience by the art object" (499). Aesthetic experience "provides the energy for further action" (503). "The courage implicit in aesthetic experience will be used to encourage unremitting effort to resolve the particular problems and to overcome the particular difficulties in science, in morality, in art, and in the practical activities of life" (504).

This theory is interesting in so far as it lapses into an error which is the very opposite of that of "immanent meaning". The autarchistic interpretation of artistic values results in absorbing the ends of art in its means, which leads to formalism. On the contrary, the absolutism of the subject's response degrades these means to more or less arbitrary stimulants and leads to emotionalism. Both theories misconceive the referential character of artistic meaning.

L. Garvin, *The Paradox of Aesthetic Meaning*, Philos. and Phen. Res. 8 (1947), 99-106, tries to save both the self-enclosed and the referential character of artistic meaning by assuming that "what an art work means, aesthetically, is simply the feeling-response obtained from it in aesthetic contemplation" (104). But an object can hardly be said to "mean" a response. The author regards the art object "as the potential symbol or bearer of emotional awareness" (106). This sounds like a revival of animism.

The problem of artistic meaning and truth has been amply discussed by J. Hospers, *Meaning and Truth in the Arts* (Chapel Hill, 1946). He defines artistic meaning as "meaning to us" (75), which brings him dangerously near to the pragmatistic position mentioned above. He is content with saying that art conveys "ways of perceiving the world which are fruitful in experience" (226), and he asks: "Would not the attitude be the same even if there turned out to be no 'reality' at all?" (231). But could there be "enrichment of experience itself" (238), if this experience did not refer to an objective aspect of reality? The author indeed admits such a reference, for he defines artistic truth as "truth-to things" (162). Yet this notion of truth-to as distinct from truth-about does not seem to be very helpful. The characters of a novel may be "more revealing of human nature than any individual persons we have met" (163), but the novel cannot achieve this result "by simply *being* true-to human nature" (206). A true artist has something to say *about* his subject-matter, his revelations presuppose a specific point of view which they invite us to share. This is more than "simply being", it is interpretation. Accordingly, art gives us something else than "acquaintance with things" (235 ff.); it is not the aim of a poem or a painting to make us "feel more intensely (once again) 'the felt qualities of experience ' " (206). A mere intensification of other feelings would soon dull our sensibility.

34   For references and more examples of composers who were inspired by non-musical subjects, see J. Portnoy, *A Psychology of Art Creation* (Chapel Hill, 1942), Ch. II, and R. E. M. Harding,

An Anatomy of Inspiration[3] (Cambridge, 1948), 82 ff. It is true that the ultimate result of composition may no longer have any connection with the original inspiration. This point has been emphasized by M. C. Nahm, *Aesthetic Experience and its Presuppositions* (New York, 1946), 332 ff. However, we should be careful in judging such cases. Miss Harding (*op. cit.*, 84, 128) gives the following quotation from the biography of Carl Maria von Weber: "Sublime mountain scenery ... might give birth to a droll capriccio, a joyous sunrise to a melancholy adagio, a grotesque object to a grave motivo"; she rightly remarks that the artist, who "sees 'a combination of things' not merely a scene as such", may have actually experienced capriciousness, melancholy, and gravity in the scenes themselves.

On the interpretative character of music cf. the important remarks by Th. M. Greene, *The Arts and the Art of Criticism*, 332-338. However, in his paper *Meaning in Music and other Arts*, Journ. of Aesth. and Art Crit. 5 (1947), 308-313, the author, without definitely making his choice, throws some doubt upon his previous views and suggests the possibility that the composer merely exhibits his subject-matter, i.e., man's emotions, moods, and conative impulses. In the preceding note I have already remarked that such a mere exhibition is not likely to arrest our attention and to give us a feeling of enrichment.

So I cannot agree with J. Hospers, *Meaning and Truth in the Arts*, that musical compositions such as Debussy's *Reflets dans l'eau* "serve to *remind* us of, or evoke in us the *impression* of, certain scenes or objects or events in nature and life" (43), and that such evocations are a subjective matter (47-48, 233). If it is true that the composer wanted to *interpret* nature or human life in a musical way, it is essential to our understanding that we should follow this intention, and not merely take some associations into the bargain.

See also S. K. Langer, *Philosophy in a New Key* (Penguin ed. New York, 1948), Ch. 8: "On Significance in Music", especially p. 191: "Because the forms of human feeling are much more congruent with musical forms than with the forms of language, music can *reveal* the nature of feelings with a detail and truth that language cannot approach". However, her discussion of program music does not satisfy me; the assertion that "if a composer's musical idiom is not so rich and definite that its tonal forms alone are perfectly coherent, significant and satisfying, it is the most natural thing in the world that he should supplement them by the usual, non-musical ways of expressing ideas of feeling to ourselves and others" (p. 196) seems to me to underrate the interpretative possibilities of music.

36   The interpretative function of art is advocated e.g. by F. L. Lucas, *Tragedy* (London, 1927), 54: "The only consolation (of tragedy) is the utter truthfulness: we have seen for an instant through its mists the sheer mountain-face of life", Denis de Rougemont, *Penser avec les mains* (Paris, 1936), 206: "Que la poésie ne soit plus uniquement cet angélisme 'démoniaque', cette nostalgie de l'infinie ou des passions que rêvent les faibles, mais un acte de présence, d'information profonde du réel", J. J. Martin, *America Dancing* (New York, 1936), 105: "Not representation but interpretation is (the dancer's) business, his duty to nature itself; the abstracting into essences of those deep-rooted experiences of human living which appearances, surface truths, naturalism, cover and deny", Th. M. Greene, *The Arts and the Art of Criticism*, 229: "The true artist has never conceived of art as an escape from reality into an ivory tower. He has attempted to come to grips with reality in his own way ... From primitive times to the present creative artists have offered us in their art a series of interpretations of human life and of man's physical and spiritual environment", D. A. Staufer, *The Nature of Poetry* (New York, 1946), 119: "Poetry is not poetry if it does not offer us a world that appears fresher, or clearer, or more comprehensive. It must understand and make us understand. It must communicate and convince. Whether its subject be trivial or cosmic, it must interpret". See also the quotations given by Hospers, *op. cit.*, 173 ff., 244 ff.

36   The paradox of artistic creation as something both identical with, and different from, its model is well illustrated by a quotation from E. G. Wolff, *Aesthetik der Dichtkunst* (Zürich, 1944), 435: "Die künstlerische Gestaltung bedeutet eine Neuschöpfung der Welt, d.h. sie hat Offenbarungscharakter in bezug auf die Wirklichkeit, weil in ihr ein realer Sinn einerseits unverändert als solcher besteht (ein Baum ist auch im Bilde ein Baum), anderseits aber neue sinnliche Gestalt gewinnt". The idea of "re-creation" combines in a peculiar manner the autarchistic claims of aesthetic purism with the naive conception of artistic representation as a copy.

J. Hospers, *Meaning and Truth in the Arts*, 50, says: "The tree is represented in the painting. It is there—before us in the work itself; representation here does not consist in correspondence with (imitation of) some object outside the work". However, the very impression that the thing "is there in the work itself" is caused by a naive acceptance of imitation. This conception of imitation is mingled with the idea of autonomous creation, from which arises the hybrid notion of "representation-*in*". That the author has not been able to free himself from the popular point of view, is apparent from his contention that "as the degree of imitation becomes less and less, that which is imitated becomes less and less the 'model' which is copied and more and more simply a stimulus to the artist or foundation from which the rest was built through his creative imagination" (41, cf. 20). Slavish imitation and arbitrary imagination are the rocks on which art threatens to split; it may steer clear of them by the compass of interpretation.

Printed in the United States
By Bookmasters